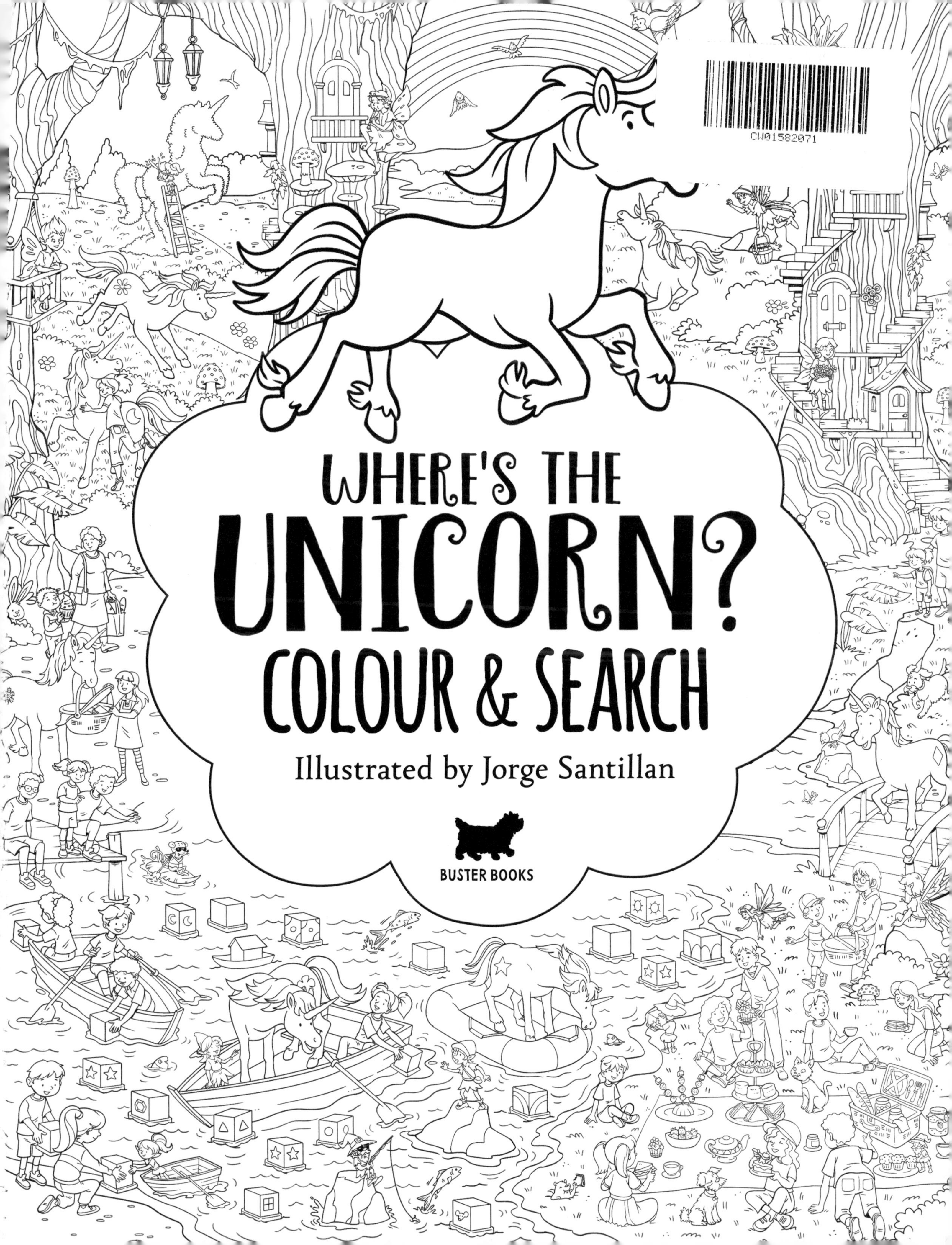

WHERE'S THE UNICORN? COLOUR & SEARCH

Illustrated by Jorge Santillan

BUSTER BOOKS

Written by Josephine Southon

Edited by Imogen Currell-Williams

Designed by Derrian Bradder

Cover design by Angie Allison
and Moesha Kellaway

First published in Great Britain in 2025 by Buster Books, an imprint of
Michael O'Mara Books Limited, 9 Lion Yard, Tremadoc Road, London SW4 7NQ

www.mombooks.com/buster Buster Books @BusterBooks @buster_books

A CIP catalogue record for this book is available from the British Library.

ISBN: 978-1-83725-020-2

1 3 5 7 9 10 8 6 4 2

This book was printed in February 2025 by
Shenzhen Wing King Tong Paper Products Co. Ltd.,
Shenzhen, Guangdong, China.

FSC www.fsc.org MIX Paper | Supporting responsible forestry FSC® C010256

Introduction

The seven unicorns of Rainbow Valley are travelling all over Fairy Land and beyond!

In every enchanting place the unicorns land, there are cute creatures and items to search for shown at the top or bottom of the scene. Colour in each one once you've found them in the picture.

Once you've spotted and coloured in everything you need to search for, you can colour in the rest of the scene.

Your magical search-and-colour adventure is about to begin ... grab your colouring pencils and dive right in!

Coral Kingdom

The unicorns are meeting fascinating creatures in this underwater paradise. Can you find the items on the opposite page in the scene?

1 clam

2 baby turtles

3 starfish

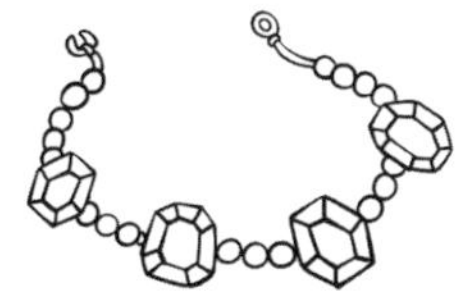
1 jewelled necklace

Rainbow Bakery

The unicorns are enjoying some tasty treats at the bakery.
Can you find the kitchen items on the opposite page in the scene?

1 bunch of
bananas

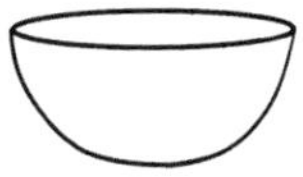

3 mixing
bowls like this

2 slices
of bread

2 pies

1 unicorn
cookbook

Toadstool Garden

The unicorns are exploring the magical homes of fairies. Can you find these enchanted items?

10 toadstools

1 gnome

At the Aquarium

Unicorns can breathe underwater!
Can you find these sea creatures
in the scene?

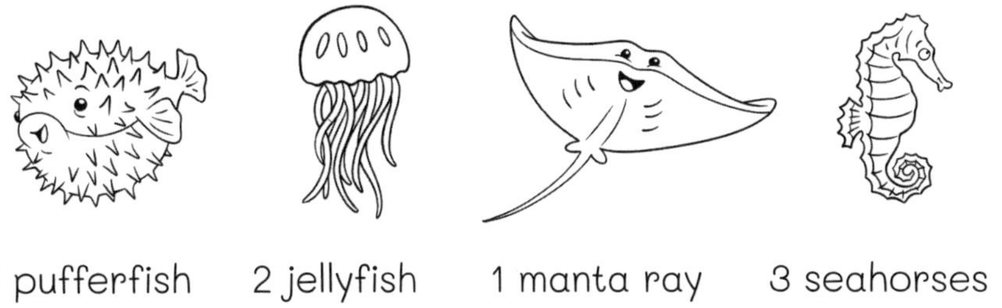

3 pufferfish 2 jellyfish 1 manta ray 3 seahorses

Haunted Castle

The unicorns need to keep their wits about them as they explore these haunted halls. Can you find the items shown on the opposite page in the scene?

1 cat | 5 spiders | 2 bats | 1 grandfather clock

Pool Party

Summer has arrived and the unicorns have been invited to a fun pool party. Can you find the items on the opposite page in the scene?

1 straw hat

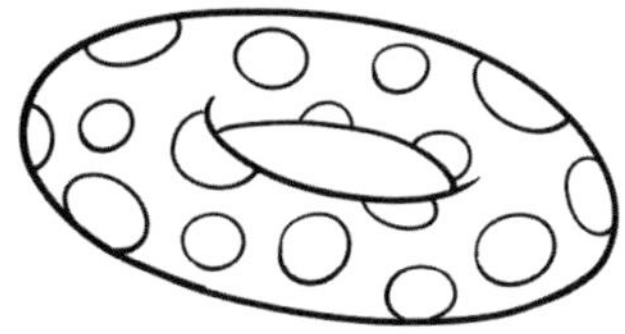

1 spotty rubber ring

5 sundaes

Land of the Dinosaurs

The unicorns have travelled back in time to watch dinosaurs walking the Earth. Can you find the items on the opposite page in the scene?

3 fern leaves

4 dinosaur eggs

1 pterodactyl

Dog Show

Dogs hop, leap and jump for medals at this competitive show. Can you find these things?

1 dog dressed like a unicorn

5 rosettes with a dog icon

4 bags of dog treats

Pirate Ship

Ahoy there, unicorns, it's time to set sail! Can you find these things?

1 map

1 parrot

1 chest

White-Water Rafting

The unicorns are feeling adventurous, and have decided to take on the rapids. Can you spot the items on the opposite page in the scene?

1 baseball cap   1 camera   3 pairs of sunglasses   1 squirrel

Victorian Steam Train

The unicorns have stepped back in time into a bustling Victorian train station. Can you spot the items on the opposite page in the scene?

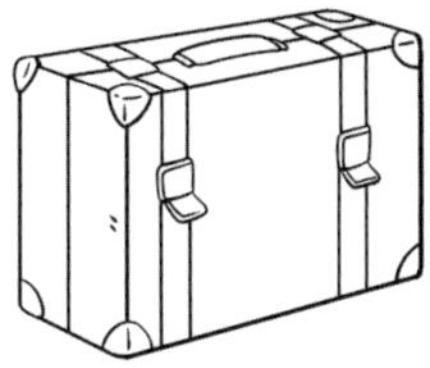

This suitcase

1 lost ticket

2 parasols

Dance Party

It's party time and the unicorns shake their tails on the dancefloor!
Can you spot the items on the opposite page in the scene?

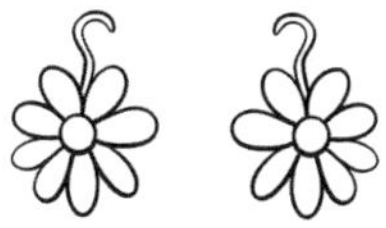

1 pair of flower earrings

1 pair of sunglasses

1 tassel handbag

Unicorn Academy

Unicorns and riders are in training at this magical school. Can you find these items in the scene?

1 half-eaten apple

1 helmet with this pattern

Dragon BBQ

These dragons are firing up the coals for some tasty food. Can you find these items in the scene?

9 burgers

3 bottles of ketchup

Unicorn Hairdressers

For the perfect unicorn hairstyle, look no further than this glitter-filled hair salon. Can you find the items on the opposite page in the scene?

1 can of hairspray

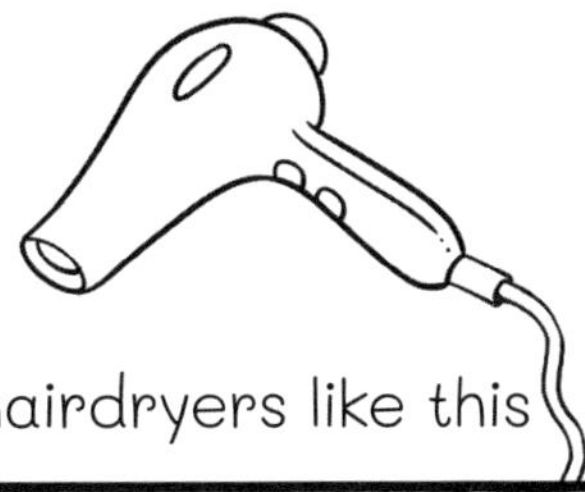

3 hairdryers like this

5 hairbrushes like this

Lantern Festival

The unicorns are taking part in a magical lantern festival.
Can you spot the items on the opposite page in the scene?

This gnome

1 lantern with an apple on it

This magical fairy

Night at the Museum

This museum has come to life and prehistoric creatures are breaking free! Can you spot the items on the opposite page in the scene?

1 old-fashioned camera

1 map

1 baby dodo hatching

Waterpark

Children race and fly down the slides at this fun waterpark. Can you find these items in the scene?

4 beach balls

1 sunhat like this

Icy Antarctica

Brr! It's chilly in Antarctica, but these animals love the winter wonderland. Can you find these items in the scene?

5 seals like this

This snowflake

Picnic Time

The unicorns are enjoying delicious sandwiches and cakes on the green. Can you find the items on the opposite page in the scene?

1 mole

5 cupcakes with a flower on top

1 jar of strawberry jam

Tropical Beach

The unicorns are relaxing in the sun on this tropical island.
Can you find the items on the opposite page in the scene?

1 dropped ice cream

1 pearl necklace

1 sandcastle with a flag in it

4 starfish

Fairy Meadow

This country meadow is buzzing with flower fairies, bees and butterflies.
Can you find the fairies and little creatures on the opposite page in the scene?

1 ladybird

3 butterfly fairies

2 dragonfly fairies

Magical Parade

All sorts of magical creatures are taking part in this enchanting parade. Can you find these items in the scene?

5 striped balloons

1 bejewelled crown

Art Gallery

This gallery is every unicorn-lover's dream come true. Can you find these items in the scene?

3 headsets

1 sketchbook

Futuristic Voyage

The unicorns have travelled far into the future to a world full of robot animals. Can you find the items on the opposite page in the scene?

1 robo-dog

1 robo-unicorn

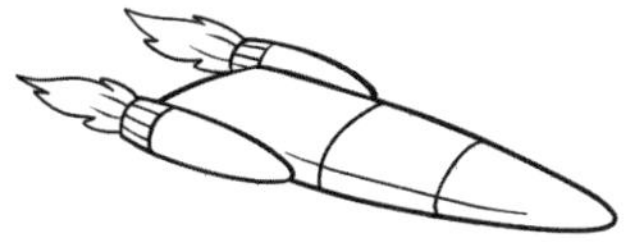

6 hoverboards

Enchanted Library

Magical folk travel from far and wide to read the best books on spells and potions. Can you find the items on the opposite page in the scene?

This book

4 hats

2 wands

Unicorn World

A unicorn-themed funfair — what could possibly be better?
Can you find the items on the opposite page in the scene?

1 mascot

1 dropped ice cream

1 box of fries

Wizard's Workshop

Magic fills the air as potions bubble and brew. Can you find these items in the scene?

1 broken test tube

This toadstool

4 pairs of glasses

Circus Night

These circus acts are getting ready for an entertaining evening. Can you find these items in the scene?

1 palette of face paint

3 toffee apples

5 juggling balls like this

Dragon's Lair

Families of dragons have made these castle ruins their home.
Can you find the items on the opposite page in the scene?

This diamond

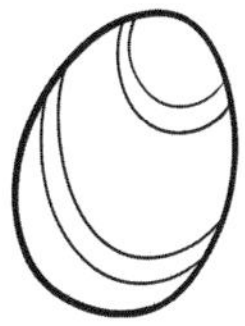

This egg

1 hatching dragon

Italian Restaurant

The unicorns are filling up on pizza, pasta and ice-cream sundaes. Can you find the items on the opposite page in the scene?

5 bowls of spaghetti

1 swan napkin

1 pepper mill

Jungle Time

This jungle is brimming with life — even the plants are talking to the unicorns! Can you find the items on the opposite page in the scene?

4 frogs

This giant toadstool

3 flowers like this

Answers

Coral Kingdom

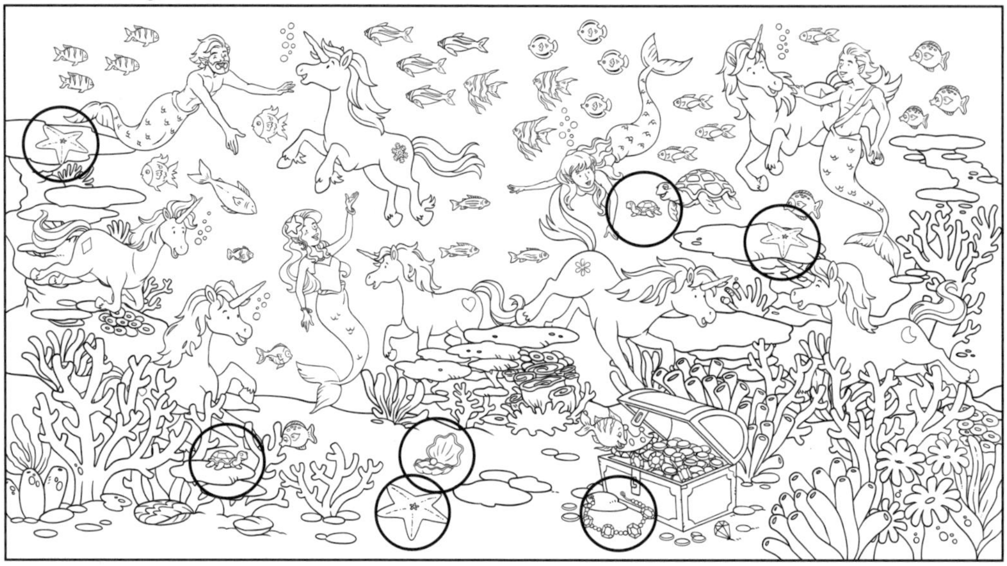

Rainbow Bakery

Toadstool Garden

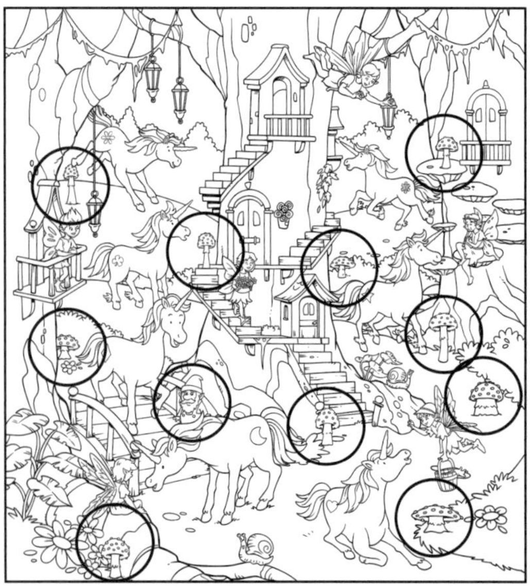

At the Aquarium

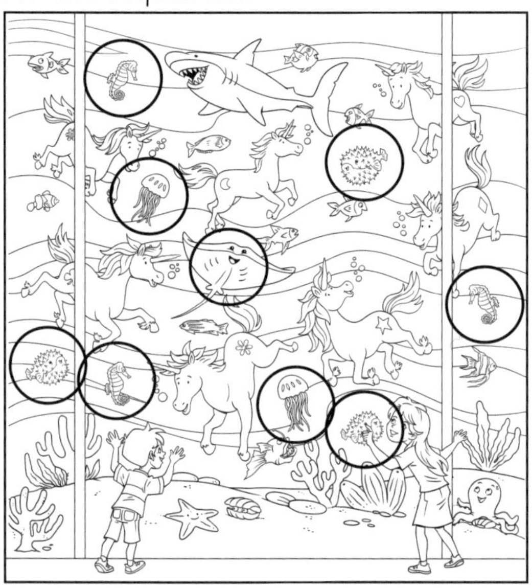

Haunted Castle

Pool Party

Land of the Dinosaurs

Dog Show

Pirate Ship

White-Water Rafting

Victorian Steam Train

Dance Party

Unicorn Academy

Dragon BBQ

Unicorn Hairdressers

Lantern Festival

Night at the Museum

Waterpark

Icy Antarctica

Picnic Time

Tropical Beach

Fairy Meadow

Magical Parade

Art Gallery

Futuristic Voyage

Enchanted Library

Unicorn World

Wizard's Workshop

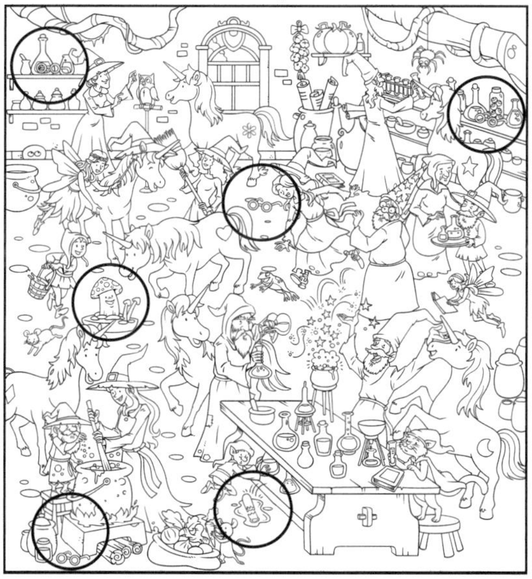

Circus Night

Dragon's Lair

Italian Restaurant

Jungle Time